15

DISCARD

Out the window it goes...

Shakespeare

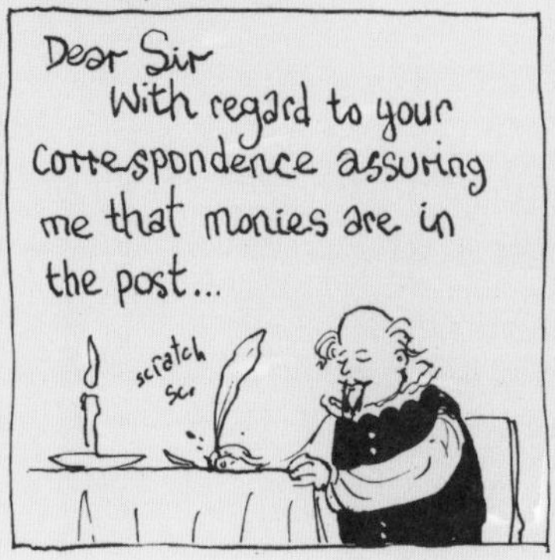
Dear Sir
With regard to your correspondence assuring me that monies are in the post...
scratch
scr

THE LOVELY HORRIbLE STUFF

my book

~ *about money* ~

by

Eddie Campbell

1

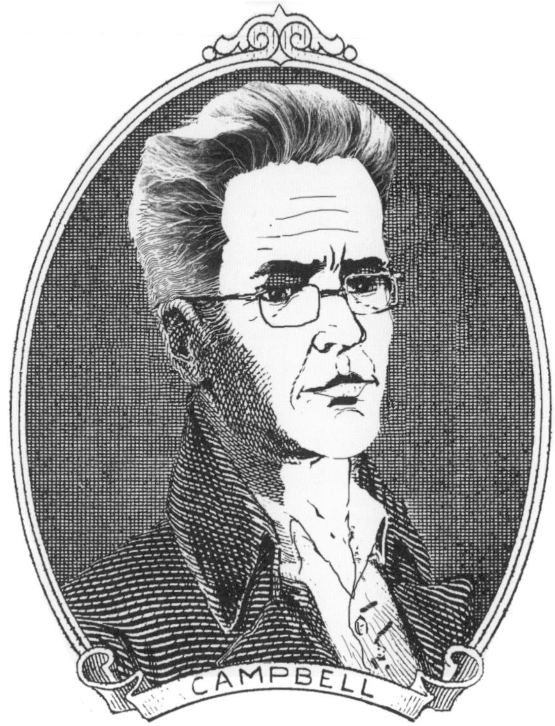
CAMPBELL

and how he got that way

Somebody said that the first sign of middle age is hair growing out of the ears.

The second is talking about money at the dinner table.

For an afternoon I was going to call this the HISTORY OF STUPIDITY, but that would give the wrong impression.

For I've always been the most sensible person where the 'stuff' is concerned.

TIME IS MONEY.

It's a maxim that has tended to annoy me.

An obstacle in the path of the daydreamer.

oi! Time is Money

Who one day might find that his 'idle daydream' is worth a great deal.

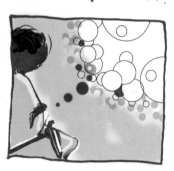

And then he'll replace the old maxim with a new one: MONEY IS TIME.

How much are we worth? About twelve months

Because this daydreamer has been made cautious by having plenty of time to think about money purely theoretically.

Money and how it gets that way.

Henry Miller 1938

He measures his value by how long he can stay up after the ladder holding him has been kicked over.

6

Air blows hot and cold in the time of intellectual property.

And the dependence on unseeables ceases to be a terror only after it becomes a way of life.

Or the circle of life, or its merry-go-round.

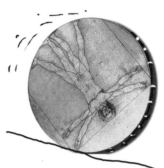

Because what does he do with all this time he keeps piling up? Why, he uses it for more daydreaming.

He doesn't need to save it for vacations, for they're already sewn into the material.

He gets around a lot of places. He just needs to sign a bunch of books when he gets there.

Even if he paid the fare himself, between tax deductions and assorted frills, it all evens out.

And it's not like he's taking time off for this gadding about, since his head goes with him.

Sometimes the wife of his bosom comes too, but I'm getting ahead of myself.

he daydreamer resents the world's making him think far too much about money.

Furthermore, Mr. xxxx, a green voucher from six weeks ago, and a blue one from four, also remain stuck in your great big teeth.

TYPE TYPE

Clearly I have trusted far too much in your crafty new colour-coded voucher payment system.

TYPE TYPE

I attach a sketch of one of my colour-coded turds. This one is BROWN.

yours etc.

TYPE TYPE

The most creative part of the creative life is coming up with persuasions to get overdue cheques.

Do you think all artists and writers in history had to do it?

I'll ask them at the café tonight.

hmm – I'll have to go out.

I thought the café Guerbois was in your head?

The one in my head has run out of beer.

Hey, Bill!

There's something I want to ask you.

8

Don't you think it's absurd that the creative life is so taken up with writing letters just to get the money that's already been earned.

Eddie 'tis truth indeed that you speak.

So many of my finest phrases have been recommissioned into the service of debt collection.

For example - ahem! THRICE you have promised me that said monies will arrive... tomorrow, and tomorrow, and tomorrow.

"...creeps in this petty pace from day to day..." — from MacBeth!

Here's another: You say the monies have 'already been sent. Well. So have I heard and do in part believe it.

HA! that's Horatio, from HAMLET!

However, such niggling discomposes us; we lose patience.

Until we cannot but unleash our fury extempore...

Oh be thou damned, inexorable dog!

Thy currish spirit governed a wolf, hanged for human slaughter.

Even from the GALLOWS did his fell soul fleet

AND INFUSED ITSELF IN THEE!

FOR THY MEANNESS is WOLFISH, bloody, starved and ravenous

But wait! There's more.

Perchance monies have been sent before your receipt of this letter...

What do you think of the soliloquy from my new play?

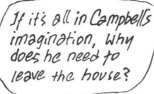

It doesn't make sense. Is it taking place in the real world, or just in Campbell's head?

What do you mean?

If it's all in Campbell's imagination, why does he need to leave the house?

Perhaps he only imagines that he's leaving the house.

Look, let me put it another way: Is Shakespeare visible to the other characters?

Yes, of course he is, Gareth.

But he's a figment of Campbell's imagination, yes?

I guess you can say that.

Look at it from OUR P.O.V. WE've got to sell it to the network.

And no TV audience is going to accept it the way you've got it here.

What do you mean?

It's like this: When we see it from Campbell's P.O.V. ...

...We should see Bill.

Then when we cut to somebody else's POV...

Campbell should be talking to an empty space.

That makes Campbell look like a nut-case.

I've got a bigger problem with Shakespeare anyway. See, you've got him using fancy words...

hm.

But that's the very thing that he's supposed to do, so it's not really funny, is it?

You see, we need to play against expectations.

What else would he use?

How about... head-butts!

now THATS funny

Hold on a minute!

Hey, Bill!

'Tis best to weigh the enemy more mighty than he seems.

Okay, m'dearie — outstanding accounts!

Aubrey's late again.

Let's do a variation on the 'slippery stool' — Dear Aubrey, you are —

TYPE TYPE

I'm watching a goanna and it makes me think about money.

In my mind's eye it looks like the one off the old dollar bill, introduced here in 1966 when the currency went decimal.

The Federal Reserve Bank decided to adorn the note with indigenous art and the designer employed an assortment of images from photos, presuming them all to be culturally and temporally remote.

The composition at left turned out to be the work of a contemporary artist still in his thirties, David Malangi.

Caught in an embarrassment, the Reserve Bank offered him a thousand bucks, a fair deal.

And they pressed him a special medal.

Malangi bought a boat with the money and proudly showed his medal for the rest of his days.

The goanna motif remains generic and/or anonymous.

Here comes another.

Now they're going at it.

My goodness, it's rough.

I think he's murdered her.

But then, after several very long minutes, she gets up and walks away.

I read yesterday that the Australian indigenous Art industry is worth 250 million bucks a year.

The old dollar bill was replaced by a coin in 1984. The one used here cost me four bucks last week. I keep the receipt for a tax deduction.

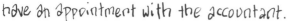

I have an appointment with the accountant.

Killing twenty minutes, I recall the first visit seventeen years before.

Did you read about that accountant who got the prostitutes a deduction for condoms?

Never mind that it's illegal, but the government is still taxing them on the earnings-

Logically, he argued, they are therefore entitled to deductions for expenses, including condoms -

The accountant-Brian- he's the one I see for my tax returns- I mentioned him to you before —

His specialty is artists and the creative industries - film, theatre, indigenous art. YOU should see him.

Honeybee, we're switching to a new accountant this year. I've made an appointment -

Artist   accountant

"Brian will see you in a minute. Please take a seat."

"There are two things I always tell a new client..."

"One: do as much of the assembling and counting as you can yourself before you bring it in."

"Two: never spend money just because it's a tax deduction."

"All very logical"

"Oh oh - brown alert!"

"It's coming out the sides!"

"The bathroom is next door left."

"- etcetera. One last question: My comic is about Bacchus, the god of wine. Can I get a deduction for my booze?"

"No."

"Are we nearly done?"

I got a gig writing and drawing a one-off Batman book through an unpredictable series of connections.

First I conducted and published an in-depth interview with a man who was a ghost-artist on the character from 1947 to 1953.

Thus I let the world know that I keep my childhood fondness for those old comics

It's not something I went looking for. In fact, I turned down an invite.

Why?

I don't do that kind of story.

I made the mistake of mentioning it to my pal White.

I've got ideas you could use.

So we wrote a 48-page Batman comic for DC Comics of New York City.

It gets complicated.

Nothing could make me happier than to illustrate this myself.

Well, that's off. They said a creator can't both write and draw the same job without being incorporated. Must be a legal condom.

Incorporating isn't as difficult as you think. A company is just a box of papers you can keep under the bed.

My pal White is in fact a practising chartered accountant and he obtained for me an off-the-shelf company.

> $1,000 official fee, and you get my bit for nowt - just so I can write Batman

> Here's the cheque.

Companies are required by law to be uniquely named and they do this by hitching a couple of unrelated words together. Well, that's my explanation.

> Antelope Pineapple Pty. Ltd.

My pal White came up with a combination sure to embarrass me, and ran the check to confirm its uniqueness.

> And I can keep it under the bed?

> You and Anne are now registered company directors.

> Just so I can draw Batman.

I further compounded the matter by asking to paint it. This opened the door on a new phase for me.

Publishing my monthly black and white comic out of the front room of the house was behind me.

Now I was making books painted in full colour, bound in hard covers or else 'french flaps'.

I was getting a nice advance for the job and then losing myself in my own head for a year at a time.

Three or four years puddled by like this in the life of

Mr Antelope Pineapple

a r t i s t

ARS SUPRA TIT

However, the company soon became an unwanted burden.

> It's a pain in the arse.

I have a hard enough time remembering one set of tax duties and obligations

> I'm getting rid of it!

Without having to remember a whole other set.

> This was your chance to save money.

For instance, I now had to think of myself as an employee of the company

ANTELOPE PINEAPPLE INDUS

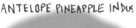

And at the same time, as company book-keeper, I had to remember the employee superannuation deadline.

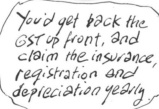

More than once I (the company) was fined for missing it

> This is what you SHOULD have done: buy the new car in the company name.

> You'd get back the GST up front, and claim the insurance, registration and depreciation yearly.

> Of course, Anne'll be up for Fringe Benefits Tax, but if you drive more than 15,000 km p.a.... and make petrol a private contribution... you'll still be ahead.

It's not too late. We'll novate the lease to the company. We'll get Dan to draft a novation agreement.

...before you need to lodge your next Business Activity Statement.

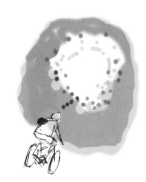

Are you seeing Brian Tucker today?

Yes—I want him to get rid of the company for me.

Do you still have that old thing?

Yes. I imagine getting out of it will be more involved than getting in —

And there will be a bunch of things for you to sign.

Erin, can you drop me in town on your way into work?

new gleam.

gleam

gleam

I'm killing time having a cup of tea, thinking of Bruce Wayne in a 1939 English tea room in our Batman comic.

Outside the tearoom there's a blackboard with a quote for today chalked on it.

"Reputation = character minus what you've been caught doing" —Michael Lapoce

Brian will see you in a few minutes. Please take a seat.

Brian!

Eddie. How are you?

—etcetera, so is that everything I have to do to get out of it?

Yes. I did once say a company wasn't for you.

But is that true? You incorporated so you could draw a Batman comic.

Yup.

That's funny— but cool.

Now, do I have to hand over the box of papers from under the bed?

Uh...no, you can keep that.

22

hey want to describe my family as 'dysfunctional'

I knew you wouldn't like it - but this is for TV.

And a normal well-adjusted family isn't good comedy.

Gareth, I'm the most conservative guy you'll ever meet. I'd go so far as to say I'm old fashioned.

Why do I have to sit down at the dinner table every single night? None of my friends have to do it!

Because it's a grand old tradition; and I like it!

And another thing, Erin.

After you left school you sat on the sofa for eight months.

Can't this wait?

And here you are now, a hard-working young lady with your Tiffany bracelet and your Louis Vuitton handbag-

Yeh, so?

Your dinner's getting cold.

23

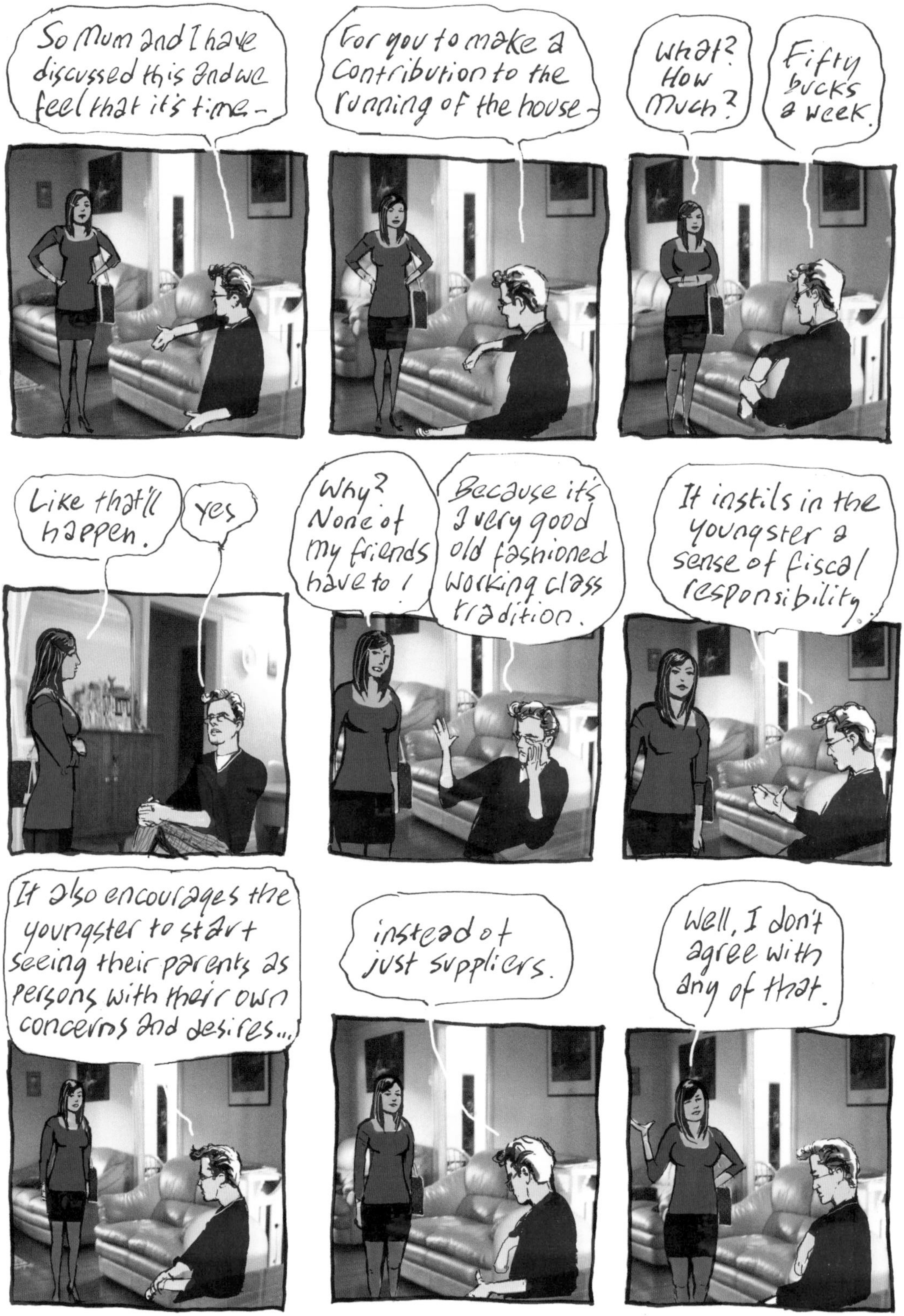

So Mum and I have discussed this and we feel that it's time-
For you to make a contribution to the running of the house-
What? How much?
Fifty bucks a week.
Like that'll happen.
Yes
Why? None of my friends have to!
Because it's a very good old fashioned working class tradition.
It instils in the youngster a sense of fiscal responsibility.
It also encourages the youngster to start seeing their parents as persons with their own concerns and desires...
instead of just suppliers.
Well, I don't agree with any of that.

It's not like I just brought the subject up. We've been on about this for weeks.

It's not too late. We'll novate the lease to the company. We'll get Dan to draft a novation agreement.

$50

All you think about is MONEY! Well HERE IT IS THEN!

Right! You won't be using the car to go to work! Give me the Key!

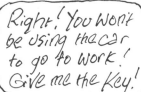

No!

Give me the car key!

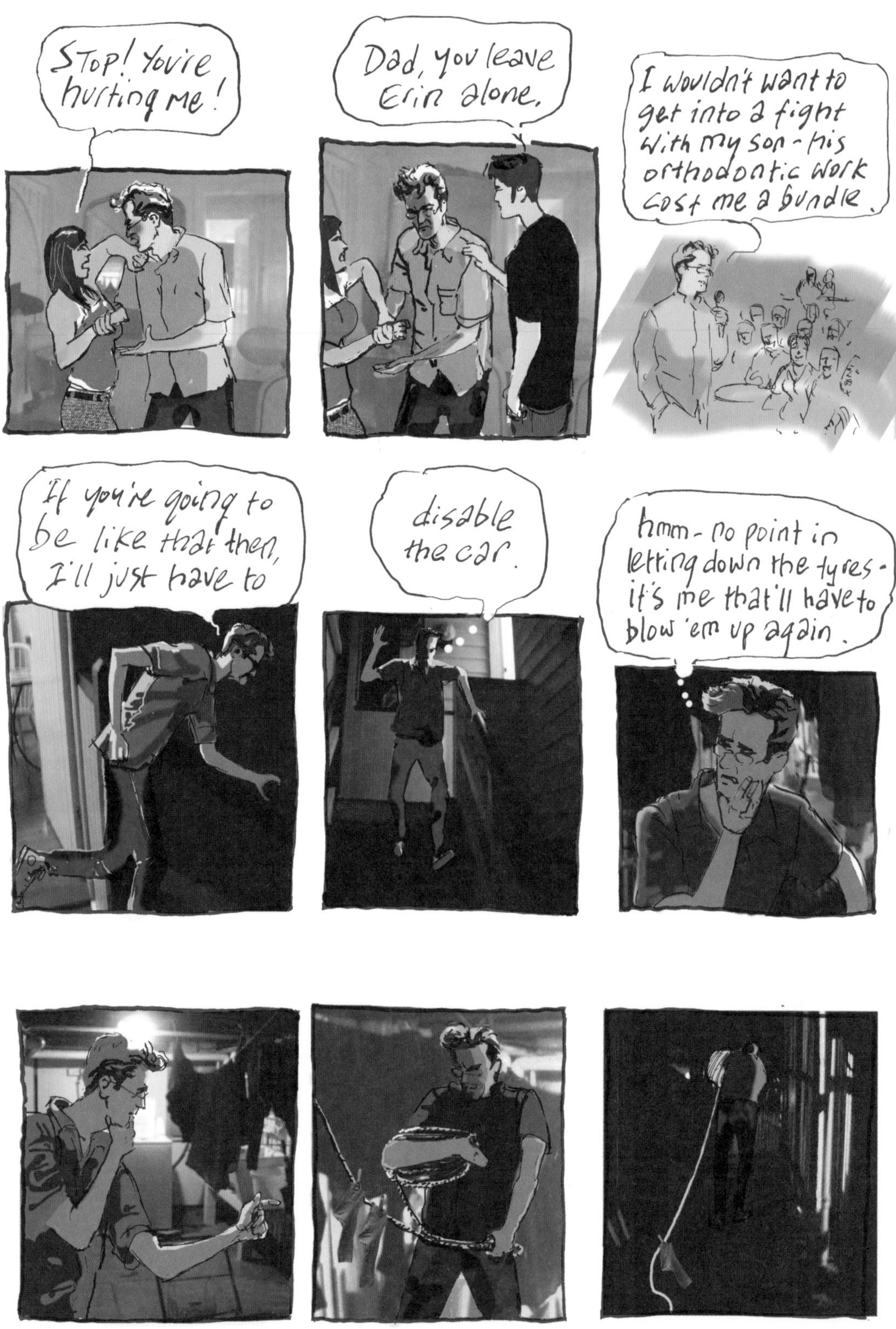
Stop! You're hurting me!
Dad, you leave Erin alone.
I wouldn't want to get into a fight with my son - his orthodontic work cost me a bundle.
If you're going to be like that then, I'll just have to
disable the car.
hmm - no point in letting down the tyres - it's me that'll have to blow 'em up again.

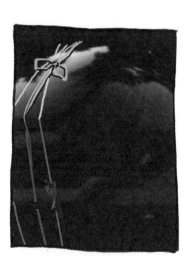

Eddie,
STOP!!

I've dealt with it.
Now take the rope
off the car before
somebody sees.

27

We spend two days shooting a two-minute demo film in which Campbell plays himself, the wife plays herself and a guy in a specially made costume plays the Snooter.

We've just added some tricky animation...

when suddenly...

The world recession arrives —

Wall St.'s Turmoil Sends Stocks Reeling

September 15, 2008
In the last two months, the chaos has taken a vicious turn. Three of the five biggest American investment banks have failed or been bought since March. Plunging housing prices have also crimped consumer spending and slowed the overall economy, which has lost 700,000 jobs this year. Even so, investors have generally seemed hopeful that the economy would avoid a full-scale recession. Now that confidence may be fading

The proposed comedy series based on Campbell's books

was an attractive proposition.

which swiftly raised development funding.

And so, development got under way...

In which Campbell resigned himself to the task of murdering his most precious ideas.

Such as the notion that an artist in his head imagines that he communicates with his mentors from the past...

Which formulated itself into the image of a metaphysical cafe where the creative individuals of history...

Still drop in from time to time,

There is no room for delicacy where comedy is concerned.

In fact he would have murdered many more to get the job done.

The proposed show, in the end, is a pricey affair, with animation and graphic effects.

And circumstance has priced it out of the market.

What didn't help was the
network's comedy dept's
scandal over a skit
about child cancer
patients.

Nor the consequent
sacking of the head
of the department,

the imaginative person
who had signed us
up for development.

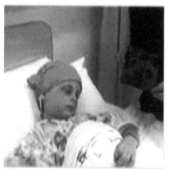

head of comedy

rolls over sick

children sketch

June 11 2009

A conservative position
is resumed. Safe
purchases are the
order of the day

local versions of
shows already
successful
elsewhere

Perhaps we'll never
see Shakespeare
headbutting
the producer.

**AUSTRALIA: Jobs
go as recession
deepens**

12 April 2009
But labour force figures released
by the Australian Bureau of Statistics
on Thursday revealed the global
recession was impacting on the local
jobs market. The figures showed the
unemployment rate increased from
5.2% to 5.7% last month while the
number of people in full-time work
fell by nearly 40,000 and the number
in part-time jobs rose slightly.

Or the Snooter giving
Campbell his nocturnal
proctological —

And the other assorted
daydreams that might
have filled his bank
account.

I know that was about
prostate check-ups.
Sooner or later you'll
have to turn yourself in

**Recession slows
climate change
progress: Obama**

Thursday, July 9, 2009
The global recession has slowed progress
on a climate change deal, but leaders must
"fight the temptation toward cynicism" and
push forward, President Barack Obama told
a meeting of rich and emerging powers in
L'Aquila, Italy, on Thursday.

But never mind the money - Campbell was picturing yet another new phase in his career,

In which he gets to act it all out and be a funny personality on television,

A raconteur on chat shows, and not just to explain what a 'graphic novel' is -

Comedy.

It's

all

---

in

the

timing.

he debt problem: not having any.

I meet my money adviser for lunch.

Hey, Lee, I've got a demand for $1,797 from a debt collection lawyer.

Is this the problem with the electric company? I told you that wasn't going away.

Yes, they phoned me nine times but wouldn't talk as I refused to give my ID details.

Now i find out that they think I owe them money —

It seems like yesterday he was 21, submitting a few stories to the monthly comic book I published.

bowl cleaner

It was in fact 13 years ago that he took a box of his Lizard Man comic to sell at a Sydney convention—

He didn't own a credit card to present on arrival at the hotel.

And so he suffered the indignity of seeing the bar-fridge removed from his room before he was allowed in.

In that moment of humiliation he vowed that he would find out all about this credit thing.

I swear by the dread Dormammu

He looked at his fine art certificate from the technical college. Then he packed in his day job at the men's clothing store and got work at a bank's call centre.

From there he somehow worked his way up to State Loans Manager governing two billion annual turnover.

This was due, in large measure, to creative problem solving and 'thinking outside the box'.

So this young chap, who took care of his father's funeral in that same Lizard Man year, is the one I ask about credit.

What can they do? Send big guys round?

Nothing like that. They'll just give you a bad credit rating.

But you absolutely don't want to let that happen.

What's the worst then?

The worst is that you'll never be able to borrow money.

But I don't believe in borrowing money.

Well... you've got nothing to worry about then, do you?

The man with nothing to worry about can't get to sleep.

either a borrower nor a lender be.

I give you Campbell and his father-in-law, a lawyer of some fifty years experience. They appear to be rational people.

Oh no, Eddie — you can never get anywhere without borrowing.

But that appearance will swiftly unravel, as you will see.

It is my opinion that we are entitled to list among our achievements any of life's accidents that fall in our favour.

Naturally any mishaps that affect us would therefore be our sins.

The first words my future father-in-law said to me:

My Dad wants to say something to you —

Eddie — if you ever harm a hair of my daughter's head, you will find that the world is not big enough to hide in —

?

He said what?

now embarrassing

I'd say it was a small town mind except that the citizens of that town did not generally think enough about the world-at-large...

To be chronically concerned about a Jewish plot to take it over.

You should spend more time in the real world, Eddie, then you'd know what's going on.

It's an odd little place, which this whimsical old-fashioned wine label often brings to mind.

Where the young folk are referred to as 'the boy—' and 'the girl—'

I see the boy Reitano is home from College—

I heard the girl Williams has taken up with an artist in London

Can you imagine what her father will have to say about that?

Father-in-law had a firmly held view that one should marry a person from one's own small town.

To marry an outsider would be a dangerous leap in the moral dark.

An artist with no money—

I'm an artist. I have no money. Well, not back then, I mean. And I've always presumed that others have a better grasp of the subject.

Father-in-law had a big house, a boat. Also, a swimming pool.

It wasn't until much later that I started to think I saw cracks in it.

He borrowed a hundred thousand to build the big house and lamented that when interest rates soared he wound up repaying a quarter million.

Most curious, this trust in the monetary system, this rosy outlook on human progress, fostered presumably by the post-World War II boom...

This certainty that we will not all be living in a third world long before the fossil fuels run out...

This belief that there is a god who has it all under control, which requires a degree of self-deception...

Grown in the trouble and expense of getting his middle son's marriage annulled...

So that it never happened, "regardless of civil ordinance, or appearance to humans"

It was definitely a marriage - you should have seen the cake.

By the demise of the second one he could no longer deny it was a divorce.

By that time his daughter and I had married outside the church and mother-in law wasn't speaking to us.

For long he held out hope of transubstantiating that bogus marriage into a real one.

You know, you can still renew your vows in the church.

Yeh, that'll happen

His dealings in real estate always ended badly. With the big house, he commissioned its construction on a beachfront...

Where the sea is infested for the whole of summer with box jellyfish

("among the most venomous creatures in the world")

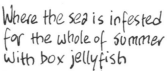

He took a dive on the resale.

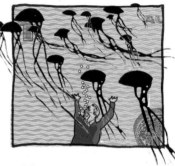

A subsequent domestic arrangement saw the in-laws buying a house with the middle son.

They all fell out and in a way it was the son's third divorce.

From this debacle, the in-laws retreated to a retirement village.

The series of mishaps had whittled down their stash considerably...

So that their financial shortfall, for getting in, equalled, with all the inevitability of high tragedy...

The exact value of our helium balloons.

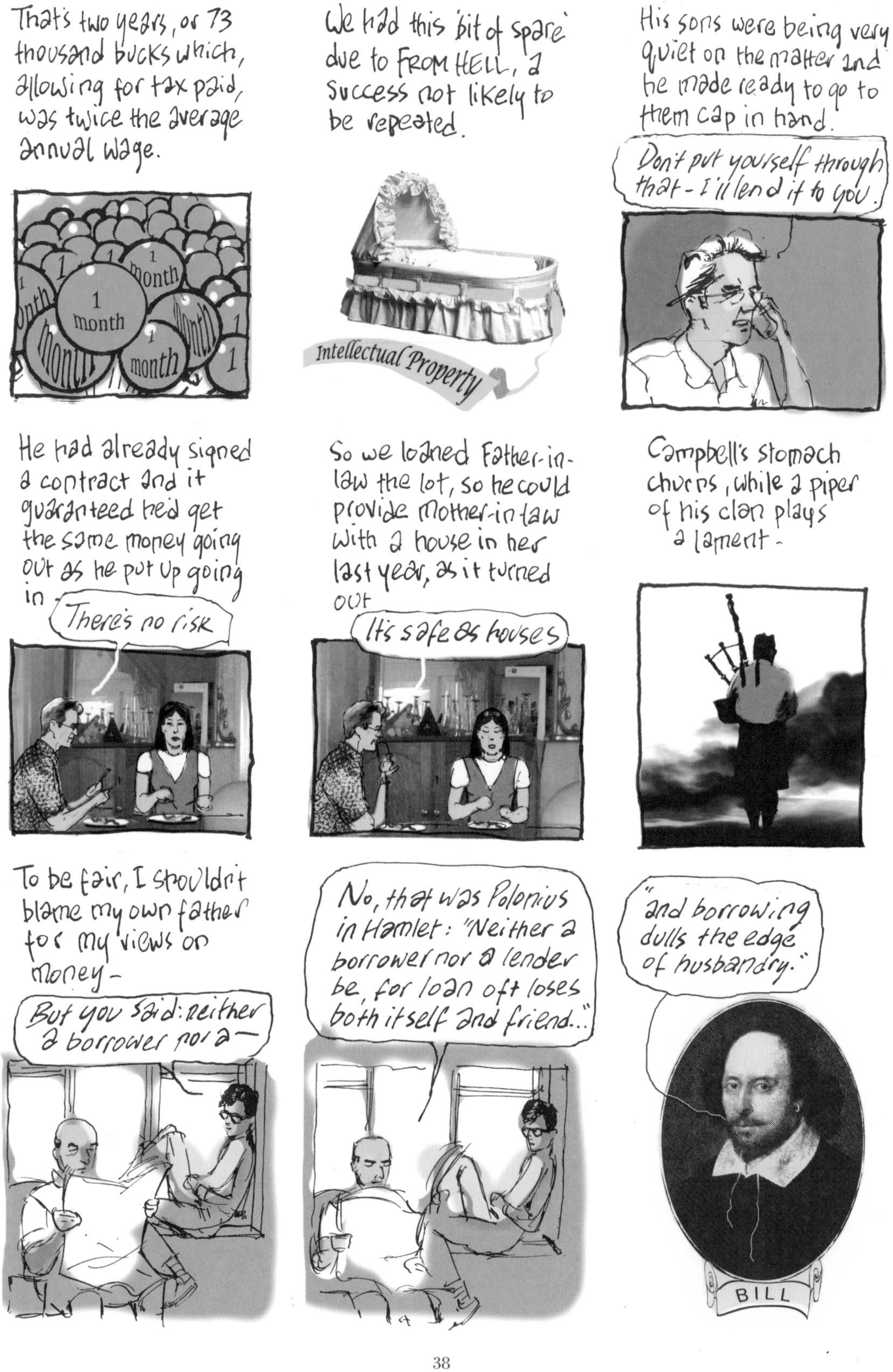
That's two years, or 73 thousand bucks which, allowing for tax paid, was twice the average annual wage.
1 month
We had this 'bit of spare' due to FROM HELL, a success not likely to be repeated.
Intellectual Property
His sons were being very quiet on the matter and he made ready to go to them cap in hand.
Don't put yourself through that - I'll lend it to you.
He had already signed a contract and it guaranteed he'd get the same money going out as he put up going in -
There's no risk
So we loaned Father-in-law the lot, so he could provide Mother-in-law with a house in her last year, as it turned out
It's safe as houses
Campbell's stomach churns, while a piper of his clan plays a lament -
To be fair, I shouldn't blame my own father for my views on money -
But you said: neither a borrower nor a—
No, that was Polonius in Hamlet: "Neither a borrower nor a lender be, for loan oft loses both itself and friend..."
"and borrowing dulls the edge of husbandry."
BILL

Seven years go down the throat of Chronos, with Ananke measuring out the portions.

Seven years, cordial and convivial.

Meanwhile, Father-in-law has gone over the Retirement Villages Act of 1999 a squillion times.

Always he confirms that the establishment has contracted to itself more than it is legally entitled.

And that he in fact should receive the full resale value of the house and not just the return of the amount he paid for it

> It has tripled in value.

It's a matter of interpretation -

> And if there's one thing I know, it's interpretations.

It's much too subtle for me

> see?

> No - but what would I know?

How a lawyer of fifty years experience signs his way into such an ambiguity in the first place is never explained -

The proprietors offer to settle with an extra $100,000, but he's not having any of it.

> I will win because I'm right.

> But didn't you ever see Dirty Harry?

Here's a picture of money blowing out the window. You'd stop it except it's such an eye-catching composition.

Where it goes: first he purchases a barrister's opinion, for which the going rate is $10,000. He concludes that the guy has no spine.

I really don't see it.

Second, it goes to court. His own barrister is doing the work as a favour, but the judge rules against him and orders him to pay the other side's costs of $50,000

They had agreed to each cover their own costs, but the other side is hardly going to object. Surely it's not the first time it's happened.

Third, wrongly thinking that the other side has engaged senior counsel, the highest level of advocacy, he also springs for one.

To his horror, senior counsel's fees come in at $30,000. The toll stands at $90k, which has to come out of his part of the house-sale...

The $160,000 sitting in a trust account through the year of disputing.

Nov 14, 2008

World recession deepens

Credit crisis worsens ahead of Washington G20 summit
PARIS - THE blast of recession hit Europe on Friday as leaders from more than 20 rich and emerging countries headed for a crisis summit in Washington. The EU announced that the 15 countries in the eurozone were in recession for the first time ever, with a 0.2 per cent contraction in the second and third quarters. Italy reported it was in recession, Spain reported its first quarterly contraction in six months and the Netherlands said it had gone through six months of zero growth. France narrowly avoided joining Germany and Britain in recession.

Father-in-law smoulders in his rented room.

They mustn't be allowed to get away with it.

The crooks!

40

Suddenly realizing it's my money blowing out the window, I phone Father-in-law.

I'm concerned that you may be about to let us down

Eddie, I would never let you down

The wife of my bosom has a go, pleading with him to give it up, but there's a rushing in his ears.

No, he's going to appeal the court's decision. The wife may never speak to him again –

It has gone beyond my knowledge of etiquette. Is there a correct way to castigate one's father-in-law?

gaaaa

In our society, money customarily pours down-wards, from deceased estate, to age, to youth.

With the young folk, dosh is spent cyclically, continually replenished by Friday's pay-packet.

In adulthood the same folk may run a business, buy a house, educate their children, invest for the future, juggling it all at once.

In old age, their world shrinks. If they have no money to pass down, they strive to put enough aside so no-one will be out of pocket for the funeral.

funiplan

They will have long ago accepted that the world no longer belongs to them.

An alternative Universe: Father-in-law's house is sold and he walks in with a bottle of champagne and a cheque for $73,000

This one: he lodges an appeal and the money, what's left of it, sits in the trust account for a whole second year.

Judges are not of the quality they used to be he says, as though judges are separate from the system they implement.

I recall the letters he wrote to his daughter when he hoped to dissuade her from attaching herself to me.

"Eddie does not hold life to be sacred."

And the letters he writes to his local paper:

"you parade the debased morals of our times on your front page..."

"...In the image of a sportsman and his de facto wife with their illegitimate child.."

Eddie - that child is a BASTARD.

The world doesn't hold that against anybody any more.

Rubbish

From over here I can hear the rushing in his ears-

Our confrontation then, if he is to be stopped, must be epistolary.

Surely he must know that's what I do -

TYPE
TYPE

An assassination by mail. Very unpleasant but I have an obligation to my own people.

I must close myself away. Lock out everything except that damn rushing in my ears.

Dear Father-in-law

I'm putting this in writing because you have made it impossible by phone to get past social pleasantries

It seems that you have no idea how angry we are at you for sabotaging a perfectly good arrangement.

Particularly we are angry that you have put us in a position of demanding repayment that we know you can no longer meet.

You have given no thought to our interests in this matter, so obsessed are you with —

But he does not reply. I try to figure him out. Is it pride? Is all that he IS, and has been, contingent upon one last win in the court-room?

You took the rewards of our labour in a hazardous trade, and you put them in the pockets of legal scoundrels

You had the insensitivity to do it in the middle of a WORLD RECESSION with our children all of college age.

But he does not reply. Is it an inability to admit he's wrong? God knows he may be right in a legal sense, but he must have known the risk.

I am returning your card sent for our 25th anniversary Please send no MORE of these bogus pieties. Save your prayers and masses.

Is it entitlement that motivates him? Does he feel that we all owe him?

You are poisonous, but not like a snake, more like a stagnant pool, dangerous only to those who FALL IN.

Is it just senility? Has he lost all concept of a world outside his head?

The Crook.

44

Five letters, no replies. The appeal goes up and another judge rules against him and orders him to pay costs again.

He hangs up when I call and I show no interest in an exchange of social niceties

Somehow $73,000 turns up in our account. Whom he had to get it from I do not want to know.

It is followed by a letter in which he remarks upon the travesty of justice and laments my immaturity...

As well as my lack of the intelligence with which I once credited you

The finish is perhaps caused by my series of maniac letters, or it just chooses to ignore the 25 years the wife and I have been married.

Though of course he may never have counted it a proper marriage.

With perfect symmetry, his final words to me are a reiteration of his first:

If you ever affront my daughter's dignity, you will find me a formidable foe—

We're in a hotel near Lucca in Italy.

We wake up to a wide view of olive groves.

I chase the wife of my bosom around the bed until she catches me.

I recall that life with the dear girl used to be like this all the time.

When we talked about sex instead of money at the dinner table.

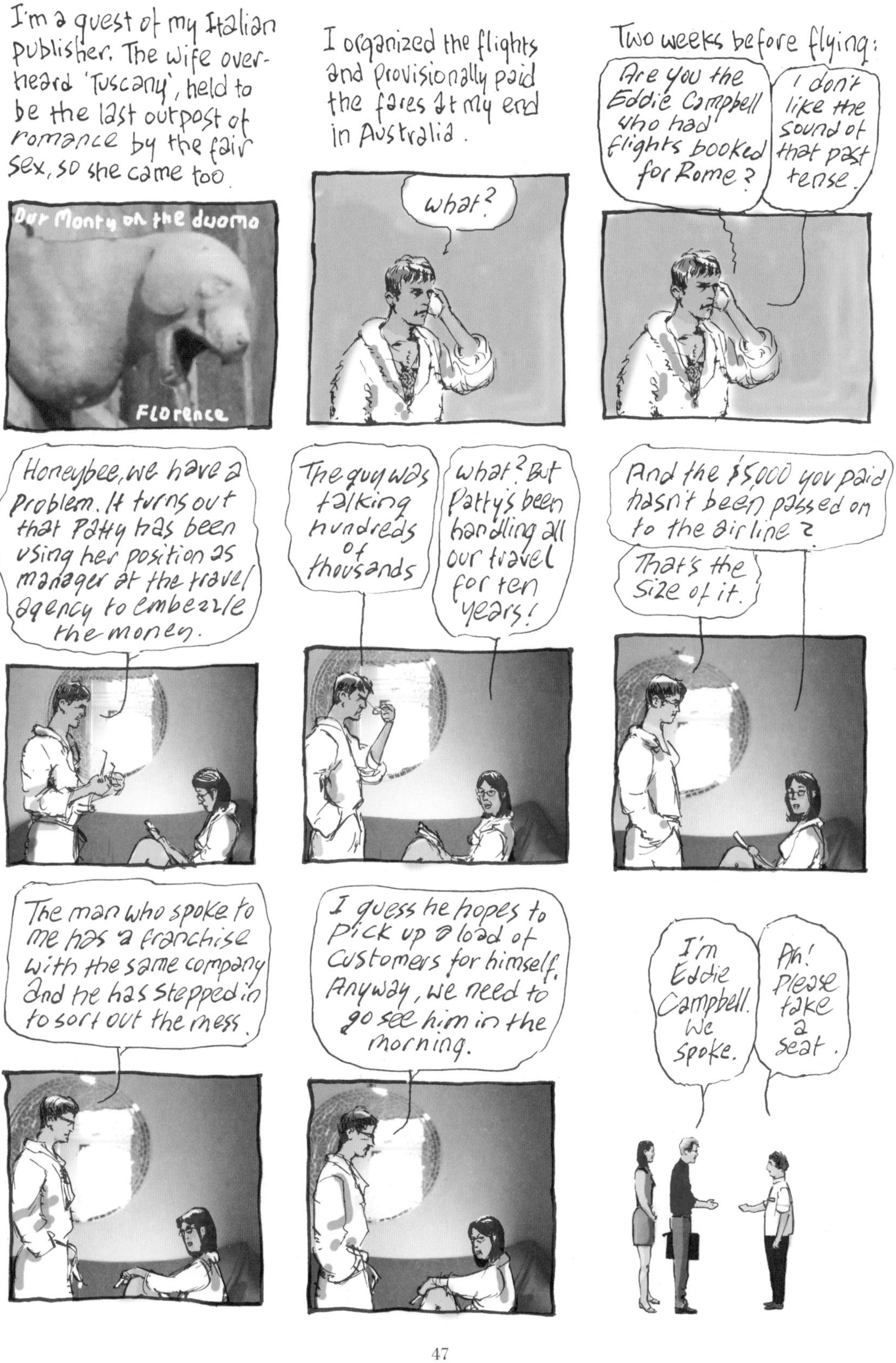
I'm a guest of my Italian publisher. The wife overheard 'Tuscany', held to be the last outpost of romance by the fair sex, so she came too.
Our Monty on the duomo
Florence
I organized the flights and provisionally paid the fares at my end in Australia.
what?
Two weeks before flying:
Are you the Eddie Campbell who had flights booked for Rome?
I don't like the sound of that past tense.
Honeybee, we have a problem. It turns out that Patty has been using her position as manager at the travel agency to embezzle the money.
The guy was talking hundreds of thousands
what? But Patty's been handling all our travel for ten years!
And the $5,000 you paid hasn't been passed on to the airline?
That's the size of it.
The man who spoke to me has a franchise with the same company and he has stepped in to sort out the mess.
I guess he hopes to pick up a load of customers for himself. Anyway, we need to go see him in the morning.
I'm Eddie Campbell. We spoke.
Ah! Please take a seat.

"I must say this is all a bit unreal." "We're still reeling from the extent of it."

"I'll be tied up for at least another week working it all out." "Do you know where she's hiding?"

"Oh she hasn't gone anywhere. She's still at home. As soon as I'm finished here, then charges will be brought."

"I pictured it like a crime movie, with her doing a runner." "Oh dear no. She has a kid at school."

"And her husband?" "He knew nothing - quite extraordinary."

"I wonder what made her do it - the Recession?" "No. It was just greed. She was driving around town in a BMW, carrying a Gucci handbag."

"She swallowed a handful of pills, but it wouldn't have been enough to soothe my bad back."

"Well, at least she knew the protocol."

"I wonder how a person gets into such a muddle in the first place." "I'll tell you."

It would start with a customer who pays in cash, say a couple of thousand.

There would be the temptation to pocket that and then use the next customer's cheque to cover the first purchase.

I see. And everything just shifts along a place —

What do they call it? a Ponzi scheme.

So you don't get caught; the sky doesn't fall. you might try it again. Everything moves along two places — And again...etc.

So what was her downfall?

Such a scheme, as I'm sure you must know, depends upon business continuing to come in at a steady, or faster, rate —

—And suddenly we're in a recession. People are not traveling as much —

Exactly. There wasn't the cash flow to cover travel that had already been booked and it all caught up with her.

Mr. Campbell, have you ever heard the saying 'desperation is the mother of invention'?

Yes? Well, every Friday she had to deposit the week's takings in the company's central account.

She found that she could deposit the cheque in the morning. The company would have counted it by midday...

But then there was a window of opportunity during which she could cancel it before close of business.

After the third time she did this, alarm bells went off at head office, who called the owner —

—on my clearance your bank will be able to claim the insurance and also reverse the charge on your card account

What happened, honeybee? Did you wrap up the business?

Yes—everybody knows when you've left the building.

Eddie Campbell 11/'09 to 4/'10

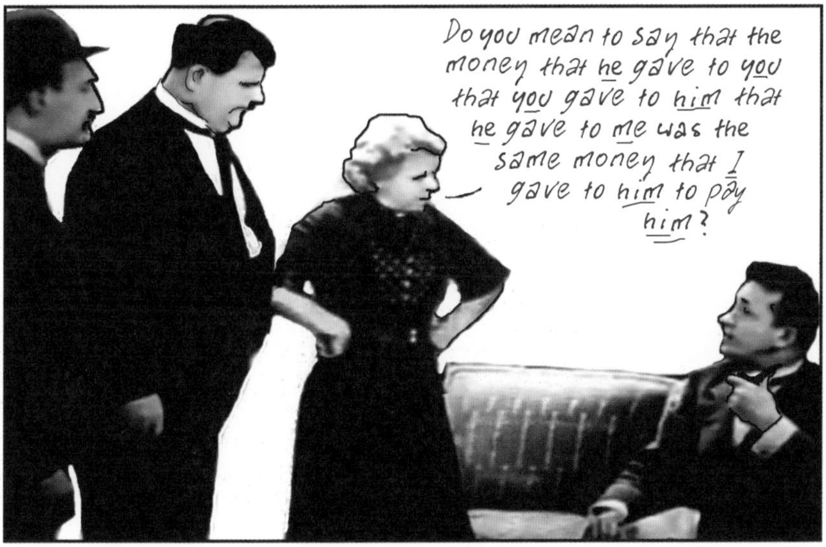
Do you mean to say that the money that he gave to you that you gave to him that he gave to me was the same money that I gave to him to pay him?

YAP

ISLAND OF STONE MONEY

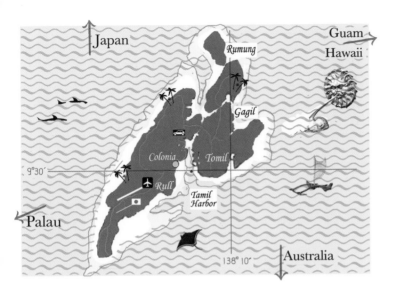

Japan

Rumung

Guam
Hawaii

Gagil

Colonia   Tomil

9°30'

Rull

Tamil
Harbor

Palau

138° 10'

Australia

It's 9° above the equator, 17 miles long, with a population of around 8,000

We've been circling the tiny Pacific island of Yap for half an hour.

It's less than 6 hours by air north of our house.

But the connections are discoordinated and it has taken us 5 days to get this far.

The island-hopping flight from Guam touches down here 3 times a week and 3 times again on the way back.

Tonight it won't be stopping here at all.

Below us, the landing lights on the runway are broken.

The 738 moves on to the next island in the chain: Palau, 250 miles southwest.

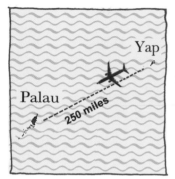

We get another set of immigration forms:

How many days do you intend to stay?

None whatsoever.

And the address where you will be residing?

I have no intention of residing

But you must give an address, sir.

There's a group of Swisses going to the same Yap hotel as we are. They're waltzing around on the luggage carts

Can the problem be solved or are we stuck on the wrong island until the next flight going back in 2 days?

A few hours later, and it's been arranged that a flight to Guam will make an unscheduled stop on Yap.

The smallest passport and customs check I may ever see.

And then a garland of frangipani is placed around my neck by the handsomest youth.

In the humid tropical night, a cool shower

Yap begins with a joke; the word means 'a canoe paddle.'

What's that yonder?

eh? that's Yap.

The Yapese live ensconced in jungle. You glimpse them from the coral rock pathways, wave and they smile and wave back.

the 'money bank' at Balabaat

The men's meeting houses are more visible, standing proudly in open space.

Upright in front of each is an imposing array of stone disks.

Elsewhere, smaller pieces leaning against family abodes, or by the road.

Yap is of interest mainly to two kinds of people: divers and economists.

"Why are you here if you're not diving?"

To the waters at the edge of the coral reef surrounding the island come divers to see the huge manta rays.

This crowd is from Poland, having their breakfast...

SCHNAYA.

aboard the Mnuw, a 100-year old Malaysian vessel put to use by the hotel as a restaurant.

There is an intensity about them, which I mistake for a toughness I would at this time attribute to diving people.

Bolsk..

Later I find that they should have gone out on the plane to Palau last night, the one that didn't come in. And now they're stuck here for two days, with their next dive taking place without them, 250 miles away.

What will they do here if they're not diving?

Outside of the handful of hotels, the buildings in Colonia, Yap's township, tend to have look of impermanence.

An enquiry at the humble Visitor's Bureau leads to an interview with John Runman of the Historical Preservation Office in the old prefab next door.

And so...but I'm getting into stories.

But stories are what I came for. I don't even mind if you make them up.

I'm neither a diver nor an economist, and the last cartoon character to come here was Scrooge McDuck in 1960.

How did the stone money begin?

The Yapese liked to travel. Or perhaps they were just caught in a storm while fishing and carried afar.

Like tourists anywhere, they'd bring stuff back, things they couldn't get locally.

From the island of Palau they brought home pieces of the bright limestone cliffs.

From the existence of a stone fish it is supposed that representational carving was first tried.

Chief, we have caught a fish for you.

And this was superceded by the abstraction of a simple disk.

To explain the disk, a satire, that the Yapese chased the moon across the sea, to catch it and bring it home.

And who would tell such a satire? They'd tell it upon themselves, apparently.

I picture it quite jolly around their campfires, burning the ubiquitous coconut husk to keep the mosquitoes away.

The disks, or rai, are made from stone not found on Yap, and are obtained at great risk.

The Yapese were among the most skilled seamen of the Pacific islands.

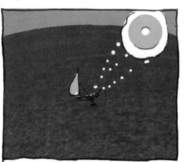

Crews from Yap used the trade winds from the northeast between January and March.

They made the five-day 250 mile voyage in their outrigger canoes with sails made from woven pandanus leaves.

For access to the limestone caverns they traded themselves as temporary labourers to the Palauans.

Then they spent the typhoon season, June to November, holed up on Palau carving rai.

Was there any tradition of stone carving on Yap?

no, just wood.

The Yapese had centuries of canoe carving expertise to draw upon.

How did they proceed? First they wedged and hammered pieces from the sides of the caverns.

They'd heated the stone and then painstakingly smoothed its surface with clamshell adzes.

Presumably a basic drill was used to put a hole in the centre to facilitate carrying

The stones were then transported to the beach and the waiting canoes.

Was there any sense of one rai stone being closer to perfection than another?

In the crafting of them, was there room for individual expression or decorative addition?

Or no more or less than we'd expect to find in an ingot?

Back at the hotel, the Poles are cooking themselves around the pool.

These tourists of the sea-bottom.

There are two girls. One is prancing through reception in a g-string.

For a woman to show her thighs in the street outside would be to give offence.

Colonia itself is smaller than the main street of the small suburb where I live.

In the street, an old woman sits in the midday shade.

Men carry their betel-nut chewing gear in little straw bags.

The hotel soap is in the shape of rai, or the moon.

A moon to chase across the sea.

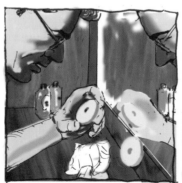

Angumang was of the village of Teab in Tomil, a trickster, some time between the beginning of time and the beginning of counting it.

huge abandoned stone disk in Palau.

He is the protagonist in versions of three different stories I picked up.

Including the one about the moon, already told.

Fad'an was his rival from the village of Ngolog in Rull-

Rival tricksters competing for the largest haul of rai.

Anqumang got a head start on the voyage. He is the legendary sailor who figured out the 'celestial compass'...

A system of 32 stars whose positions and movements he memorized.

And he understood the directional messages from the crisscrossing swells of the ocean.

Anqumang reached Palau in only five days, far ahead of Fad'an, and his men began work.

By the time it came to race back to Yap, Anqumang's men had carved a large number of stones.

Meanwhile, Fad'an and his men had carved only half as many

Fad'an decided that if he couldn't carry the largest cargo home, at least he could get there first.

A towed raft is used, for the scale of *rai* collecting has grown considerably.

(This looks implausible until you consider that the discs would work as a keel)

As he sets out to sea, Fad'an is suspicious of the way Angumang is permitting him to take the lead.

He knows Angumang is a cunning trickster. It has to be a trap.

He steers his vessel into a Palauan cove and waits.

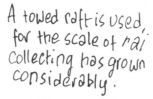

Angumang, setting out with his huge cargo, conjures an unseasonable typhoon far ahead to menace his rival.

Impatient to overtake his rival, Angumang finds himself caught on the fringes of his own storm.

With his dangerously unwieldy cargo.

As a desperate measure he cuts half of it loose.

With his lighter load he completes the dangerous voyage successfully.

The joyful greeting the men receive on their homecoming...

is marred by the people's sadness over the demise of Fad'an and his crew.

Meanwhile, in the Palauan cove at Remith.

64

Fad'an and his men wait for the storm to clear.

As they head for home they find a cargo of rai floating adrift.

Fad'an claims it.

Triumphantly, they arrive home...

To find the Poles on the upper deck of the mnuw decanting their duty-frees into their throats.

Damien the barman has gone for the manager to have them removed.

I find myself puzzled by this tortoise and hare story, in which the nominal hero snookers himself...

Until I read the version in the Yap Visitor's handbook, in which he doesn't, and in which there is no imbalance...

in the respective hauls of the rivals. Am I looking at the persistence of village rivalry?

4

After breakfast I give the British manager of the hotel a greeting. He tells me the Poles were banging drunkenly on his door at three in the morning.

God knows what it was about.

that's funny

We've hired a car for 20 bucks a day. The modern currency here is the U.S. dollar since Yap came under American protection following World War II.

Thus the American right side drive is the rule... which throws us for a loop

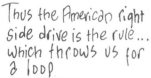

But the cars are all second-hand imports from Japan, with contrary right-side steering.

The speed limit is a low 20 miles an hour, so it doesn't matter at all.

We drive to see a 'money bank', in English, or properly a *malal*, or ceremonial ground. There are many of these around the island.

Stone money wasn't the only currency. They had shell money and other valuables for everyday trade.

Rai was the big stuff. It was wealth.

After those early adventures, there were regular outings to obtain the precious *rai*.

These were dangerous voyages. Sometimes whole crews were lost at sea.

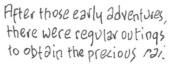

The danger of the trip and the loss of life would be reflected in a piece's value.

Though they're mostly black now, a stone's appearance would also influence its worth.

"The streaked aragonite of a brownish chocolate color and the milky white with small crystals were preferred."

The daily meals don't need to be bought. Food is swimming in the sea, rolling out of chickens- It's ubiquitous.

Rai wasn't for that. It could be exchanged as gifts with other villages, and used as payment for assistance in war.

When the rai arrived in Yap it was usually stored outside the village men's house.

The chief would make decisions about ownership of the disks.

Some might be given to individuals while others would be designated as village money.

A point to note about the larger stones is that when ownership changes, the stone isn't required to be moved.

A public ceremony is performed and the community knows who owns what.

Today the stones are covered in mould and moss. How glorious they must have once looked, with their quartzy glints catching the sunlight.

The first certain contact with Europeans was in the early 1600s

There is a legend that a chief, on the outlying island of Seepin, had a vision.

In his mind he saw white-skinned people coming in a huge craft.

The chief called a meeting of the leaders of the islands.

The chiefs of Seepin tried to press the community to a strategy of submerging the islands beneath the sea to flee from the outsider.

The debate dragged on and they could not reach an agreement.

So the leaders of Seepin tearfully broke off talks.

Seepin's magicians sank the entire island beneath the waves

Their Atlantean domain was never seen again above water.

The first permanent foreign presence on Yap was established in 1861 by a German company named Goddefroy e Sons.

Goddefroy set up a station to harvest copra, the kernel of the ubiquitous coconut, used to make oil.

The great value of coconut oil to the Europeans was beyond the comprehension of the Yapese.

It's at this point that Captain O'Keefe enters the story of the stone money of Yap.

An Irish-American castaway, he washed up on the coast of Yap in 1871 where he was brought back to health by Fatumak, a magician.

He was styled by some the monarch of Yap, as narrated in the 1950 novel

Which was played up in the 1954 movie, based on the book, starring Burt Lancaster.

O'Keefe's success in the Pacific derives from the fact that he understood what the rai meant to the Yapese.

This can't be said for the movie, whose opening legend describes them as 'worshipping' it.

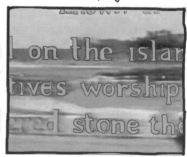

Meanwhile, the Swisses are cooking themselves around the pool.

The Poles are drinking the hotel's first-rate in-house brew. They have a new problem.

We can't get back to Poland.

This may be true. The eruption of the volcano Eyjafjallajökull in Iceland has grounded 1500 flights across North Europe.

We're stranded for two weeks! It's either here or Manila. I went to the goverment office here and demanded that they take care of our hotel bills

He says the official acceded to his demand, which doesn't sound right to me.

The captain of the Mouw invites me to fire the cannon to announce happy hour.

In goes a balloonful of divers' nitrox, off comes the nose-bag; a touch of the taper and...

BLAM!

Then the Poles get happy all over again and at midnight they bundle off to the airport.

bolski

There they all get on a huge craft and are never seen again by this author.

5

At breakfast on the Mnuw,

one of the Swiss is showing her video of frenzied, seething sharks...

Being fed from the back of the boat after the dive.

Chugging across the harbour.

I see a little girl in her father's boat,

holding a chicken

Back at the Visitor's Bureau, I ask if they can put me in touch with someone who knows about O'Keefe.

It happens that the island's expert on O'Keefe is on the premises. Don Evans is the general manager here. He's also the proprietor of O'Keefe's Waterfront Inn and O'Keefe's Kanteen, both designed by him to have an olde Worlde charm.

Don—Eddie and Anne Campbell—we're staying at the Manta Ray—

Ah—perhaps you met the Polish group.

Indeed we did.

Those poor guys were stranded here because the plane couldn't land—

They were in my office here yesterday thumping their fists on the table and demanding to be taken care of.

WE were ON that plane up there, going round and round. Do they know what caused the problem?

Nobody's admitting anything. Continental is blaming it on the contractors brought in by the U.S. government

They've been making the renovations to the runway to bring it up to Commercial standard

I wonder if O'Keefe would find entry conditions much improved?

If he was in fact shipwrecked!

That's but one aspect of the story that doesn't jibe with historical data. There's no record of a missing ship that fits time and place.

I love enthusiasm. Doris has me juggling with the anomalies in the story before I really know what the story is.

David Dean O'Keefe was a sea-captain of Irish origin and U.S. settlement. He had a wife and child in Savannah, Georgia.

Upon establishing himself in Micronesia, he acquired two more wives. The dispersal of his considerable estate was disputed for years

His descendants in Georgia tried to squash the book, which had two wives and the movie which had one, but not the white one in Georgia.

His story was in the papers shortly after his death and inspired a balonious song:

Now Jim O'Shea was cast away // upon an Indian isle // The natives there, they liked his hair // They loved his Irish smile

So they made him chief Panjandrum // the Nabob of them all // Sure i've got rings on my fingers, bells on my toes...

And Elephants to ride upon, my little Irish rose // So come to your Nabob next Patrick's Day —

However, to what is both known and relevant: O'Keefe lands in Yap as a captain in the employ of a company in cosmopolitan Hong Kong.

His ship is a renovated Chinese junk which he named Katherine, after his wife in Savannah.

His crew is Chinese also.

On Yap he establishes a trading station for Copra.

He is confronted with a native population not interested in being his work force.

He conceives a clever solution. He'll transport the Yapese quarrying crews on board the Katherine to Palau.

Where they can work with the more advanced tools he brings to bear on the situation.

Including dynamite.

75

A few months later, on his return trip, O'Keefe picks up the crews along with their hai.

The stones and the Yapese are delivered safely home.

Whereupon O'Keefe announces, not without serious risk, that he will be keeping the rai.

Or at least that he intends to hold onto it all until his copra sheds are filled.

This changes the rai collecting in more ways than one.

Firstly, most of the risk has been taken out of the venture.

Secondly, much larger stones can be carved and transported.

The disks brought home by raft tended to be not larger than three feet across, but now a diameter of as much as six feet is sought.

Thirdly, the complicated societal limitations on who is permitted to obtain rai and own it are eroded.

Consequently, the Yapese came to value the 'O'keefe money', as they still call it, less than the older rai.

The company under whose name O'Keefe traded went bust in 1875 and he was his own man from then on.

He was one of the most colourful characters of that era in the Pacific; his reputation was legendary.

David O'Keefe remained on Yap for thirty years. He brought up a large family there.

They lived in a house on an island near the harbour, once called Terang, nowadays named O'Keefe island. Only the stone steps of the house remain

He became relatively wealthy in the copra trade and added several ships to his fleet.

In 1901 he was on one of them when he failed to return from a regular trip to Hong Kong. He was presumed lost in a typhoon.

The only known photo of the man, late in years, hangs in a heavily re-stored version in the lobby of O'Keefe's Inn.

Don Evans believes that's him in a much earlier photo on the wall of the Kanteen across the road.

I wait for the musician to take a break so I can get a shot of it.

after old sepia photo on wall of O'keefe inn

⑥

The economic dimension of the *rai* stones was addressed significantly by anthropolgist William Henry Furness III in *The Island of Stone Money*, 1910. Furness collected the story told to him by Fatumak.

(Klingman and Green had O'keefe being found by the same Fatumak, on nobody's authority but their own.)

There was a family who was wealthy, but no-one, not even they, had ever seen their stuff.

It consisted of a big stone at the bottom of the sea.

Many years before, an ancestor of the family quarried the stone and was bringing it home.

Caught in a storm, the party had to let it go.

They all testified that it was a magnificent piece, lost through no fault of their own.

"It was universally conceded that the mere accident of its loss was too trifling to mention"...

"And that a few hundred feet of water offshore ought not to affect its market value."

"The purchasing power of the stone remains as valid as if it were leaning against the owner's house."

This story, of a verbal claim to a lost asset being used as money, has had an extended life in the field of economics, beginning with Keynes in 1931.

In other words, an obscure South Sea island, using money made of stone, had arrived independently at the kind of abstraction that typifies modern finance.

Milton Friedman yoked the anecdote to another from the same source in a 1991 conference paper.

WACKY WORLD OF ECONOMICS

KEYNES 9

WACKY WORLD OF ECONOMICS

FRIEDMAN 71

In 1898, the German governors of Yap found fault with the footpaths between villages and they ordered them to be repaired.

The rough coral blocks were good enough for bare feet and 'many were the repetitions of the command.'

It was decided to impose a fine and an officer was sent through the disobedient districts.

He marked a number of the most valuable rai with a black cross.

"The People, thus dolefully impoverished, got to work repairing the pathways"

To the apparently absurd behaviour in this anecdotal composite, Friedman made a comparison to an episode in U.S. banking history.

In 1932, the bank of France feared that the USA was about to devalue the dollar

WACKY WORLD OF ECONOMICS

FRB

69

It asked the Federal Reserve Bank of NY to convert its dollar assets held there into gold.

WACKY WORLD OF ECONOMICS

HEDGE

18

To avoid the trouble of shipping the stuff, France asked New York to just store it in France's account

Officials of the Federal Reserve Bank went to the vault, put the right number of ingots in separate drawers...

And put labels on them.

The headlines in the financial press bewailed America's loss of gold.

But what difference is there between labels on drawers and painted crosses on stones?

FRANCE

Or between France's belief it was in a stronger position due to gold 3,000 miles away and the Yap stone under the sea?

Others have added their glosses: Michael F. Bryan in *Island Money*, 2004, explains that Yap's stone money serves no purpose outside of just being money.

ECONOMICS
WACKY WORLD OF
BRYAN
90

What economists call 'fiat money',

a medium of exchange to solve the problem of 'the coincidence of wants'.

ECONOMICS
WACKY WORLD OF
BARTER
3

ECONOMICS
WACKY WORLD OF
COMMODITY MONEY
5

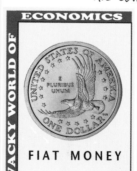

ECONOMICS
WACKY WORLD OF
FIAT MONEY
10

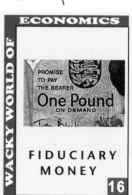

ECONOMICS
WACKY WORLD OF
FIDUCIARY MONEY
16

Others have dissented. Dror Goldberg in "Famous Myths of Fiat money" poo poos the Furness story on the basis of internal inconsistency.

WACKY WORLD OF ECONOMICS
GOLDBERG
91

The sea-disk is still owned by the family of the man who made it, has never been used in trade, and thus does not demonstrate itself to be money of any sort.

For economists, the sea-disk long ago entered the realm of parable and Yap itself is a theoretical island-state exemplar that doesn't need to be invented.

WACKY WORLD OF ECONOMICS
YAP ISLAND
39

WACKY WORLD OF ECONOMICS
$ £
€ ¥
CURRENCIES EXCHANGE
60

Figuring out whether to classify rai as 'fiat money' or the equivalent of 'gold reserve', or whatever, is on the same plane as trying to calculate an exchange rate for it.

Furness unintentionally popularized the notion that a 3-foot disk was worth a 100-pound pig.

What doesn't make sense is why somebody would go to all the trouble of quarrying and carving and shipping a stone just to buy a pig with it.

Or anything else for that matter.

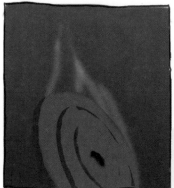

The thing to do would be to keep it in the family. This yarn of the ages. The one that got away.

I have a driving curiosity about the stones, quite apart from the economic thing

If you ask the Yapese about their arts, they'll talk of dancing and ceremonies. But as an artist, I would like the stones to also have an aesthetic dimension.

Sure, they looked grand and I covered that already, but my mind is the sort that would like to go around cataloguing the stones.

Taking measurements, writing descriptions, finding similarities, making connections.

To me these stones are sculptures. I want to identify carvers, tease out their personalities, find their stories.

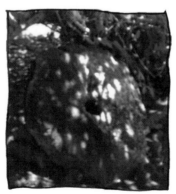

Thomas Lautz touched on this aspect of the subject in a 2004 paper, *The World's Most Curious Money?* Unlike most economics commenters, he had actually visited Yap.

To begin with, he separated the *rai* into two broadly different classes. On the one hand, large, roughly carved pieces.

On the other, those with a more polished finish, often 'stepped', and smaller in size.

Among unusual and individual pieces he found some with a decorative motif around the central hole.

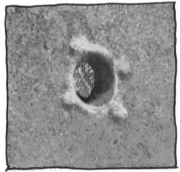

There is a prestigious stone with two holes, carved by Churen Chowon of Waryan in Gagil. One village placed itself in servitude to obtain it, then used it to buy peace between two other, feuding villages.

John Runman told me of a piece called 'the butterfly stone'. Churen Kadyed, chief of Gachpak in Gagil, commissioned two stones to be carved as one, like this

He gave a part to each of his two wives, and as the parts were inseperable, it was his plan that the two ladies would stay together as his wives.

Lautz described it as Siamese twins, lying overgrown by jungle. He asked some youths about it, but they didn't know it was there.

John told me about another pair of rivals, Fodal and Piluw, trying to outwit each other like Anumang and Fadan.

This time they were vying to cut the largest stone! According to John they each came in at around eight feet diameter

Presumably the upper limit of the Katherine's hold space.

O'keefe probably needed to balance the boat

In my initial enquiries I found two phases of rai: O'keefe and pre-O'keefe. Now another shows itself.

After O'keefe, there were late Victorian steamships of greater capacity. Larger and larger stones were cut: 8ft, 10ft...

In the great hyper-trophying of the stone money of Yap.

Rai ni ngochol is the description of a class of stones that have acquired individual names.

The greatest is Rewergurus, meaning 'twice cheerful,' so named because the chief's wife sat on it.

Which you must not do; It's disrespectful

It is the largest piece of stone money on the island, being 12ft across. I have no idea how they would move it.

The colossal stone is in Rumung and is unavailable for public viewing due to an event in the mid-'60s.

Rumung was at that time joined to the mainland by a simple bridge.

The villagers, convinced of the exceeding beauty of their place, decided to keep the tourists out, and so destroyed the bridge.

You don't think that lot had anything to do with sabotaging the runway lights do you?

ha!

I've found an article on the 'net by a writer and longtime scholar about Yap who got to look at *Rewergurus*.

He was shown it by one Tomasz, whose grandfather, Tammad, led the carving of it.

(another one kept in the family!)

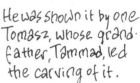

He was forbidden from photographing it.

In the pool, Anne talks to someone who says there is a way of getting to see it if you speak to the right people.

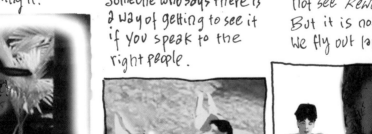

To come all this way and not see *Rewergurus*. But it is not to be. We fly out later tonight.

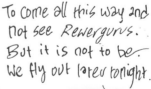

In 1919 Germany blotted its Copy-book and Japan got Yap under the Treaty of Versailles.

A Japanese census of 1929 Counted 13,281 rai stones on the Island.

By 1942 and the Second World War, the Japanese were using them for landfill to build an airstrip

And soon for boat-anchors and other purposes.

Then the USA chucked a bunch of bombs onto Yap. It must be shitty to be invaded by one crowd and then bombed by their enemies.
I imagine I see shrapnel damage on some of these stones.

You can still see the wrecks of crashed Japanese Zeros from those years.

This 1990s Mazda looks as picturesque; imagery of cars being consumed by jungle has its own aesthetic.

The last piece of rai was made in 1931

It was quarried and carved by Gilimoon of Dechumur village and given to Figir of Luwech.

Gilimoon had been exiled from Yap and, by this means, bought back his place in the community.

It too went into the landfill.

After the war, Yap fell under the guardianship of the USA. Just as in earlier periods rai found its way into museums in Germany and Japan, now it landed in America.

Washington, Smithsonian

The Information in the display of this piece tells us that Yo-v made it in 1904. He brought it to Yap on the steamer Germania. It belonged to chief Gaag of Balabat when it was sold to the Smithsonian 'with the permission of his community' in 1962.

In *The Stone Money of Yap: a numismatic survey*, 1975, Cora Gillilland catalogues 148 known *rai* stones in world museums.

She also presents the transcripts of depositions from a 1961 civil action in Yap over ownership of a stone.

A narrative summary gives invaluable insight into how the stuff was still being used in the twentieth century.

Urun and Tamangiro, from Af village in Tamil, went to Palau and got three pieces of *rai*. They gave the largest to Af village and kept a smaller one each.

Urun's house burned down and the people of Af helped him rebuild. He gave his stone to Af.

This stone was later given by Af to the village of Dechumur in appreciation, for a dance that was put on, and the stone was taken to Dechumur, where it stayed until JAN 15 1960.

Meanwhile, Tamag of Dechumur got a piece of *rai* from Palau of about the same size, and the people of Dechumur gave this to the people of Af.

They gave the other piece to Tamag, who gave it to his brother Fazagol when the latter was about to build a house.

Fazagol gave it to Puguu in payment for some tin roofing. And this is where it starts to get complicated

Choo, the plaintiff, claimed that Puguu gave it to him in 1937 as a marriage gift in return for Choo's guarantee...

to care for three children which Choo's wife brought into his home at the time of their marriage.

However, Pong, the defendant, claimed that Puguu gave it to him in 1938 in exchange for alcohol, some shell money, and assistance.

On Jan 15, 1960, Pong came round with other named men and removed the stone over the protests of Choo.

For the price of $125.00 Pong then sold the stone to the Money Museum of the

The judge ruled in Choo's favour and ordered Pong to give Choo the $125, being no small amount in yesterday's stuff.

National Bank of Detroit

By 1964 the rai count on the island was 6,600 and in 1965, legislation was enacted to make exportation difficult.

In 1986, Yap became an independent state within the Federal States of Micronesia.

The USA still chucks a bunch of dollars into the economy. I'm reading the blog-post of a US taxpayer in Guam complaining about it.

Houston

For our last day I'd been hoping to see some village dances.

I'm reading how on Yap Day one year recently, one village's traditional dance was performed by another village. Even a dance can be bought and sold on Yap.

However, the hotel can't raise the required audience numbers for putting on the show. The Swisses, faced with the problem of it being inadvisable to dive on the same day as flying out, opt for cooking themselves.

The dance and the stones reflect the same collective imagination, or culture...

a compound world that imposes upon its people as a transcript of reality...

freeing minds from limitations that teach how little our life may expand as we wished.

Their stories are no doubt full of the wise and spiritual and mythical and lovely.

I could have tapped into it more if I had given myself more than five days...

and wasn't just a trafficker in novelties.

This narrative is of adventure and risk and acquisition. It starts with rival tricksters conjuring typhoons.

And it ends, like far too many of our narratives, with two people squabbling in court.

Invariably it's over

The lovely, horrible stuff.

Today we're assailed by extraordinarily complicated monetary abstractions

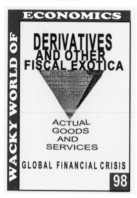

But on the way home I find my head going the other way. I'm thinking about bubblegum cards.

We'd all build a stack of them, two random cards at a time. Some were deemed to be special. It could be a cartoon character, a soccer player, a helicopter...

We'd swap them. A special card might demand several lesser ones, but letting go of a special one wasn't the end of the world...

because we were in a closed system and everything would come around again. Unless the worst happened and the kid moved to another school

Possessing a thing beyond tomorrow afternoon was too complicated to think about

A card would show the marks of every grubby hand that touched it.

I once swapped a special card for a pair of soccer boots - temporarily, for sure - and now I sported '60s stylishness

I knew the good of this could never be adequately explained to my mother, who would have done her pieces.

So I hid the boots after every game. In those days mothers did not drive you everywhere.

I never asked but have always wondered how the deal was got past the other mother.

In the backs of our noodles crouched the feeling that the balances of our system were beyond the adult mind.

A year after this naive reverie, my wife is falling out with me over money.

It's been going on for a month now.

Because you're a control freak.

And all these years, I thought I had everything under control.

I explain basic monetary theory to the marriage guidance counsellor.

you can float aloft clinging to these pink balloons, see.

or you can plunge to the bottom of the briny deep with all your currency.

Eddie Campbell 4/'10 to 5/'11

Thanks: to Wes Kublick, my oft-time collaborator of many years ago. We once made two weeks' worth of a mock 'daily strip' about William Shakespeare interminably writing demand letters for overdue money, which we thought was hilarious. However, we found that perhaps you have to be a self-employed writer to 'get it.' I have stolen a piece of the dialogue Wes wrote for it to re-use here on pages 9 and 10; to Daren White, who wrote his own accounting gobbledegook for me on pages 20-21; to Michael Eaton, for telling me about the stone money of Yap; to John Runman at the Yap Historical Preservation Office, who filled me in on the history of it; to Don Evans at the Yap Visitors Bureau, expert on the subject of Captain O'Keefe; to Anne, who was driver and factotum on the trip; to Jason Conlan, who obtained a copy of the movie, *His Majesty O'Keefe*, from Andrew at Trash Video, the place to get obscurities in this town (by the way, the cover of the paperback book I've reproduced on page 70 was painted by Warren King, a comic book artist who had moved up to illustration by 1950); to Gareth and Andrew for the adventure of trying to make a tv show out of my blatherings. If I rather cheekily made them look like antagonists here, they will know it's for the sake of the 'drama' they tried to coax out of the material. Arf!

Reading:
The Island of Stone Money, Uap of the Carolines by William Henry Furness, 1910
His Majesty O'Keefe by Lawrence Klingman and Gerald Green, 1950

All of the following can be found online in pdf:
The Stone Money of yap: A numismatic survey Cora Lee C Gillilland, 1975
The Island of Stone Money by Milton Friedman, Feb 1991
Island Money by Michael F Bryan, Feb 1, 2004
The world's most curious money? Huge stone discs used on the Micronesian island of Yap by Thomas Lautz, 2004
Famous Myths of Fiat Money by Dror Goldberg
Cultural Heritage and Communities in Palau by Rita Olsudong, 2006
The Man Who Was Reputed to be King: David Dean O'Keefe by Francis X. Hezel, SJ

The Lovely Horrible Stuff © & ™ 2012 Eddie Campbell.

Co-Published by Top Shelf Productions, PO Box 1282, Marietta, GA 30061-1282, USA & Knockabout Comics, 42C Lancaster Road, London, W11 1QR, United Kingdom. Top Shelf Productions® and the Top Shelf logo are registered trademarks of Top Shelf Productions, Inc. All Rights Reserved.

Cover designed by Eddie Campbell and Chris Ross.

First printing, June 2012.
Printed in China.